THE BATTLE

OF

THE BALLOTS

BY

HENRY CLAY MORRISON

First Fruits Press
Wilmore, Kentucky
c2013

ISBN: 9781621711254 (Print), 9781621711261 (Digital)

The Battle of the Ballots by Henry Clay Morrison
First Fruits Press, © 2013
Pentecostal Publishing Company, circa 1928

Digital version at
http://place.asburyseminary.edu/firstfruitsheritagematerial/71/

For all other uses, contact:

First Fruits Press
B.L. Fisher Library
Asbury Theological Seminary
204 N. Lexington Ave.
Wilmore, KY 40390
http://place.asburyseminary.edu/firstfruits

Morrison, H. C. (Henry Clay), 1857-1942.
    The battle of the ballots / by Henry Clay Morrison.
    40 p. ; 21 cm.
    Wilmore, Ky. : First Fruits Press, c2013.
    Reprint. Previously published: Louisville, Ky. : Pentecostal Pub. Co., [1928?].
    ISBN: 9781621711254 (pbk.)
    1. Smith, Alfred Emanuel, 1873-1944. 2. Presidents -- United States -- Election -- 1928. I. Title.
E748 .S63 M67 2013   974.7

Cover design by Haley Hill

asburyseminary.edu
800.2ASBURY
204 North Lexington Avenue
Wilmore, Kentucky 40390

First Fruits
THE ACADEMIC OPEN PRESS OF ASBURY SEMINARY

THE BATTLE

OF

THE BALLOTS

H. C. MORRISON, D.D.

25c each; 5 for $1.00; $12.50 per 100.

PENTECOSTAL PUBLISHING COMPANY
LOUISVILLE, KENTUCKY

TABLE OF CONTENTS

CHAPTER 1

The question is being asked everywhere
why was Al Smith nominated for the Presidency of these United States? This is a reasonable question when we remind ourselves
of his many limitations. He is a man of
practically no education. His environment
in his childhood was bad. His life was cir-
cumcribed. He never rose above those evil
environments. But coming into manhood,
he associated himself with Tammany Hall,
one of the most corrupt, political organizations, not only in the United States, but all
the world, with a history of graft and dis-
honest through almost a century.

It should be borne in mind that Al Smith
has never been elected Governor of the great
state of New York by the American citizens
of the state, but by the vast hords of un-
Americanized foreigners, who have gathered
by millions, in New York City, making it a
menace to the peace and welfare of this nation. If the reader will investigate he will
find that the American people out of more
than two-thirds of the counties of the great

state of New York have always voted against him.

Al Smith has been elected Governor only by a great drinking, foreign population, whose sympathies, ideals, and moral standards are entirely out of sympathy with the ideals and conceptions of the people of the northern, middle western and southern states. In many of the western states we have foreign born people of protestant countries whose industry, integrity, and excellent character, for good citizenship in these United States cannot be surpassed.

It is worthy of note that in his speech of acceptance Al Smith makes a plea for an open door to immigrants. He plays upon sentiment when he suggests that he stands for immigration laws which would not separate families. It should be remembered that nearly everybody in southern Europe could easily claim kinship with some one in this country. Governor Smith claims in his address of acceptance that there are some millions of idle workmen in this nation. The remedy he suggests would be, we suppose, to open the gates for the immigration of multitudes of starving people who are ready and eager to work, for the very lowest wages, in order to furnish the idle laborers of this country with work at good wages. Tammany

Hall has thriven, grown, and become powerful by dominating the great mass of ignorant foreigners, who raised up under the oppression of a Romish ecclesiasticism become the easy dupes of New York's political demagogues.

But we must come closer to the answer to the question at the head of this column. There were three reasons why Gov. Smith was nominated for the Presidency. First, his friends knew that he would get the entire Catholic vote. There may be a few excellent Catholic citizens who will not vote for him. But they are so very few that they are not considered. The Pope with his powerful influence, and Press, at home and in this country, and in fact, throughout the world, gives full endorsement to the candidacy of Al Smith. This is a very powerful influence. This means that the newspapers of this country knowing the intolerance of Roman Catholics, will be very careful not to make an attack upon Al Smith's candidacy. This applies to a very large per cent of our daily papers, and especially those in strong Cathlic communities.

Next, Smith's friends counted upon all the wet element of the nation, who oppose Prohibition and advocate the liquor traffic, from the millionaire distillers and brewers, to the society clubs, and down to the bootleggers and back-alley drunkards, it has been found that the worst bootleg districts always poll the strongest vote against any sort of Prohibition legislation.

Smith's advocates without any sort of question counted upon the solid south, which was necessary to secure his election, to fall into line without hesitation and march to the polls under the banner of Rum and Romanism, and vote for Smith. They believe with this combination of the solid Roman Church, the wet Democrats and wet Republicans, with the riff-raff of the cities, and the more prominent politicians, who could be bought with place and money, and the solid south, Smith could not fail of election. This is, at bottom, exactly why he received the nomination.

It will be remembered that the Smith advocates, in the great foreign city of New York, at the Democratic convention four years ago practically rent asunder the Democratic party. The great element of good and true people left that convention discouraged, dejected, alarmed, and ashamed. They were startled to find such a tremendous force in New York City, rallying under the standard of Smith, that had no sort of right to claim to be Jeffersonian Democrats. A powerful mob, under the domination of Tammany Hall, that had fought the election of Tilden, Cleveland and Wilson, had become bold and defiant enough to undertake to place one of their leaders at the head of the nation as President, for the direction and control of the destiny of this great Republic.

The Democratic party has never been able to rally its forces and recuperate its shattered and discouraged ranks, since that convention. Meanwhile, Tammany Hall, with its powerful financial resources, has worked diligently ever since that convention, preparing for the convention at Houston, which gave Smith the nomination. Not in harmony with the wishes and will of the southern people, but by powerful forces, and propaganda, that was imported south to walk rough shod over the intelligence, conscience, and ideals of the southern people.

Gov. Smith has made no sort of contribution to the advancement of American civilization. He has never written a paragraph, uttered a sentence, or performed an act that recommends him to the confidence and faith of southern Democracy. He is not the chosen candidate of the South. He was thrust upon them by a group of Tammanyites, who have opposed and fought to the last ditch the candidate under whose banner the solid south has rallied. He is the candidate of Tammany Hall, and of foreign un-Americanized, population of New York City. Southern people are in no sense under any sort of obligation to support him with their suffrage. They ought to so thoroughly rebuke the group of men that nominated him that they will learn a lesson at once and for all, that the great southern states will not be dominated by, dictated to, or affiliated with, the corrupt, un-American multitudes of New York City.

CHAPTER II.

We notice from the daily press that Governor Smith, with his secretary, and a group of friends, have been searching into the legislative records in order to find just what his attitude was to the liquor interests in his early days in the legislature. Other parties have searched into those records and found that his attitude in those days in his early political life, was exactly what it is today; the only change is his larger influence for evil. Then he voted to put bar-rooms in hotels in prohibition zones. Quite recently he secured the passage of a bill in the New York legislature which so far as the enforcement of prohibition laws in New York by New York officials, nullified the Eighteenth Amendment. His biographer, Mrs. Muskowitz, tells us that "The liquor interests were friendly to Tammany Hall; and Smith stood for legislation favorable to them which Tammany sponsored."

It is hardly prbable that the Governor's secretary wrote and published a statement of this character without his full knowledge and approval. The fact is, it was written in order to increase his influence with, and to secure the support and votes of the liquor oligarchy, and all of those who are opposed to the prohibition of the liquor traffic.

It is not necessary for Governor Smith and his friends to search musty records in order to find the contents of his telegram to the Houston Convention, in which he ignores the wishes and prayers of the best people of the Democratic party, who have voted their states free from the curse of the liquor traffic; neither need he go back to find the spirit, sentiment and language of Mr. Raskob, the prominent wet Republican chosen by him as the chairman of his campaign committee, who accepted the position with enthusiasm, declaring that he did so in order to help Governor Smith free the country from "the damnable affliction of prohibition."

It is not at all necessary for the Governor to waste time or suffer any anxiety with reference to a record on the subject of the liquor traffic which is certainly sufficient to secure him the sympathy and votes of bloated, lawless millionaires like Raskob and DuPont, down to, or perhaps, we had better say, up to the most dangerous, wicked and lawless element in the slums of our great cities. Raskob, DuPont and Smith are counting on the votes of the most dangerous classes of our American population. For the benefit of our readers we produce here Governor Smith's record in the early history of his political career, which is in perfect accord with his nullification of the Eighteenth Amendment, his telegram to the Houston Convention, his choice of a wet Republican as chairman of his campaign committee, and of what he would do if he should be elected president of these United States.

GOVERNOR AL SMITH'S RECORD.

I. Record on Referenda.

Governor Smith has been for various fake referenda and straw votes which have masqueraded under the name of referenda, but on real referenda questions he has been consistently opposed to the referendum principle. His record as a legislator speaks for itself.

1907—April 3, Voted to keep local option bill strangled in Excise Committee.

1910—April 26, Voted against amending Raines Law, so as to allow local option in cities.

1911—May 24, Voted against local option bill for cities.

—July 19, Voted against Gray local option bill.

1912—Voted against Lincoln bill to grant local option to third-class cities.

1913—Appointed eight Tammany men out of thirteen on Assembly Excise Committee and refused to give representatives of the people a chance to vote on any temperance legislation.

1914—March 19, Voted against Gillett bills to grant local option to cities, city sub-divisions and counties.

1915—March 31, Voted against Fish bill for referendum on state-wide prohibition.

—April 7, Voted against Preswick bill to grant local option to university city of Ithaca.

—April 20, Voted to kill Howard bill granting

local option to cities, city sub-divisions and counties.

2. **Record on Regulation of Liquor Traffic and its Separation From Vice.**

1904—March 18, Unrecorded on bill putting additional restrictions in the Raines Law.

1905—Voted against the Prentice bill to kill assignation houses and houses of ill-fame run as "Raines Law" hotels, thereby voting to continue infamous "Raines Law Hotel" abuses. Passed over 2 to 1 against his opposition.

1908—Voted against bill stiffening up regulatory and enforcement features of the Liquor Tax Law.

1913—As Speaker, engineered the defeat of the Knight Bill against knowingly delivering liquor in dry territory except to bona fide consignee.

3. **Record in Favor of Breaking Down Former Safeguards Against Liquor Traffic.**

1904—April 14, Voted to force hotel bars into over 300 dry towns and make hotels independent of town local option elections, and thus by robbing the popular vote of part of its effect, to nullify the town option feature of the Liquor Tax Law.

1912—Voted for Hackett bill to make it harder to convict New York City liquor dealers for violating the law.

1913—February 26, Engineered passage of McCue bill emasculating a saloon-ratio section of liquor tax law.

—March 26, As Speaker, engineered the passage of the McCue bill to save convicted liquor-law violators from revocation of their licenses.

4. **Record in Favor of Liquor Selling on Sunday and for Limitation of Prohibited Areas.**

1907—March 26 and April 23, Voted for opening up prohibited areas to sale of liquors.

1911—May 24, Voted for Walker bill increasing hours for sale of liquors.

1913—As Speaker helped desperate effort all through session to pass bill legalizing the opening of saloons on Sunday in New York

City. Engineered passage of Walker bill increasing hours of sale of liquors.

5. **Record in Favor of Permitting Saloons Within 200 Feet of Schools, and Abolishing the Prohibited Areas About Churches.**

Governor Smith has said that the saloon "is and ought to be a defunct institution in this country," but at every opportunity he ever had as a legislator he voted in favor of the saloon and privileges for the saloon.

1908—Voted for bill to remove all zone provisions protecting churches and schools from saloons.

1909—Introduced and pushed bill to permit hotel bars within church and school zones.

1911—Voted for Sullivan bill opening up prohibited zones about churches and schools to hotel bars.

1913—As Speaker engineered passage of bill permitting saloons within 200 feet of private schools.

6. **Record in Favor of Gambling and Gamblers.**

1904—April 6, Voted against the bill adding strength to enforcement features of the law against gambling.

1908—Fought Governor Hughes' Anti-Race-Track Gambling Bill through two legislative sessions, "to his lasting dishonor," the Citizens Union said.

19910—May 27, Voted against Perkins bill relating to gambling and betting establishments.

7. **Unrecorded on Bill Against Bribing Labor Leaders.**

1904—April 14, Unrecorded on enactment of measure against bribery of representatives of labor organizations, designed to prevent the laboring man from being sold out to the brewers and other special interests.

Smith Condemned by the Citizens' Union.

The Citizens' Union, of New York City, respectable, and influential, in 1907 said of him, "viciously opposed anti-race track gambling bill to his lasting dishonor." In 1909 it said he "made one of the worst records of the session." In 1911 it said that he "showed not the slightest evidence of independence, but continued his opposition to aggressive reforms. In 1912 it said, "Majority Leader Smith on most issues of importance stood against the public interest."

In 1913 it said, "Speaker Smith executed the orders of the machine. He opposed primary and election reforms." It said in 1914, "Smith and certain associates were active and able chiefly in support of objectionable measures, and seldom used their influence on the side of public interest or on behalf of desirable measures."

These appraisals of Smith were contemporaneous with the making of Smith's record. The Citizens' Union formed its judgment of Smith when the facts were fresh, not after the public had had a chance to forget them.

As Governor in 1919.

In the election of members of the Legislature in November, 1918, the ratification of the Eighteenth Amendment was a public and party platform issue. In the previous session ratification had been pressed, but had been defeated by the substitution of a bill for an illegal "referendum" on the ratification resolution, which legally impossible substitute had then been killed. The Democratic party thereafter had put in its platform a plank opposing ratification, made it a state-wide legislative issue of record, and lost the Legislature overwhelmingly. Yet when the Legislature convened Al Smith, that year elected Governor, feigned in his message that there had been no expression from the people on the issue, asked that legislative action be postponed, and advocated the same illegal and impossible "referendum" idea which was used to kill ratification the previous session. After the Republican majority, most of them elected on the issue, had ratified the amendment late in January, he said that the Legislature had seen fit to record the people "without ascertaining their wishes."

As Governor in 1920.

In his message to the Legislature in January, 1920, he argued that the Eighteenth Amendment was not yet adopted although it was already ratified by forty-five states, asked the Legislature to do the constitutionally impossible and "rescind" its previous ratification action, and again falsely contended that, "The members of the (preceding) Legislature were not elected in view of any proposed amendment to the United States Constitution," although the platform of his own political party had made ratification a state-wide legislative issue in 1918.

During the session of 1920 he openly backed the nullification beer-bill proposed by Republican Assemblyman Gillett and Democratic Senator Walker.

When he signed this nullification beer-bill he said:

"If representative Democratic government means anything it surely means that when a substantial majority of both houses makes its declaration upon a matter of this sort, it is representative of the majority sentiment of the state."

Thus the same Smith who had held that a Legislature elected openly on the ratification issue was "not elected in view of any proposed amendment to the United States Constitution" and had recorded the people "without consulting their wishes," now held that when the same body passed a beer bill, in defiance of Federal law without nullification having been an election issue, it was truly "representative of the majority sentiment of the state" merely because there were votes enough to pass it. He did not ask for a "referendum" on nullification, although that policy openly arrayed the state of New York against the Federal Constitution and Federal Statutes, which indicates that his referendum pleas were not born of any passion to learn the people's will, but only to serve the liquor traffic."

As candidate for re-election in 1920, and after the Supreme Court of the United States had killed his nullification beer-act, he ran on a platform which said:

"We favor an amendment to the so-called Volstead Act that will make operative the act passed by the State Legislature (the nullification beer-act) and signed by Governor Smith,"

As Governor in 1921.

On September 26th of this year Smith was Temporary Chairman of the Democratic State Convention and made a speech urging that the Democratic party be committed to a state law on behalf of beer and wine and the repeal of the State Prohibition Enforcement Law.

The New York Evening Telegram of September 27th further said: "It is known that former Governor

Smith made a strong declaration in the platform committee that the party should declare for the repeal of the Mullan-Gage Act." It was during the same year, on February 22nd, to be exact, that Smith was present at the New York Police Lieutenants' notorious dinner held at the Commodore Hotel, which was characterized editorially by the New York Evening Post, as "an impudent challenge to law that not even the most determined opponents of the Volstead Act can regard with equanimity." The New York Evening Telegram stated that Smith received "the ovation of the evening." There is no record anywhere that the then ex-Governor Smith had at any time indicated the slightest disapproval of the riotous and disgraceful conduct at the dinner.

As Governor in 1923.

Al Smith was chiefly responsible for the repeal of the Mullan-Gage Law. It was he who bludgeoned and coerced the dry Democratic Senator who finally broke down and cast the deciding vote for repeal. Smith did not leave anything to chance in his desire to hurt prohibition. He attended to the Senator personally. He thereafter signed the bill repealing the State Prohibition Enforcement Law, and, having taken away all the power which the state could give to its officers, he virtuously commanded the same officers to enforce prohibition under penalty of removal.

As Governor in His Last Two Terms.

During Governor Smith's last two terms his espousal of the liquor traffic and advocacy of hooch has been noticeable by its drinking modesty. He has apparently been thinking about something else. Of course, his opinion on liquor questions had been reflected in the votes of the Democratic members of the Legislature over whom he sits as czar. These votes have almost without exception been unanimously wet. Witness various memorials to Congress telling Congress what it should do to modify or repeal prohibition.

Since the repeal of the Mullan-Gage Law deaths from alcohol have mounted rapidly in New York, while at the same time in the rest of the United States, they have remained practically stationary, or increased at a very much smaller rate. The coincidence is so striking as to be almost conclusive. The responsibility for these deaths is indisputable; it is Smith's. He signed the repeal of the Mullan-Gage Law. During the last session of the Legislature he consented to the action of and abetted the Democratic membership of the Legislature, which, with one exception, voted for a resolution telling Congress that something ought to be done about poison liquor. Since the Legislature Governor Smith has been quoted as being in favor of discussing poison liquor at a medical health conference in Washington. But when two Democrats voted in a committee of the Legislature to report a bill which would punish the person who sold poison liquor, Governor Smith made these same legislators reverse themselves. He made them vote in the Assembly representing his view as a friend of the bootleggers and against legislation punishing them for selling, not just ordinary liquor, but poison liquor.

The Governor's annual message to the Legislature on January 5, 1927, was colorless enough in respect to prohibition, but he did go out of his way to call upon the Legislature to do something, which was not the business of the Legislature anyway, but of the Secretary of State, the only purpose of the act being to furnish aid and comfort to the opponents of prohibition.

His message said:

"I believe that the duty now rests upon the Legislature to pass suitable resolutions conveying in a formal manner the result of that vote for the referendum so-called to the Congress of the United States and memorializing it in behalf of the state of New York to exact at the earliest possible moment a sensible, reasonable definition of what constitutes an intoxicant under the Eighteenth Amendment so that harmless beverages which our people have enjoyed for centuries may be restored to them!"

During the past year Governor Smith has been forced to remove from office the Republican District Attorney and Sheriff of Saratoga county. Involved in the same investigation was the Democratic Commissioner of Public Safety at Saratoga, one Dr. A. J. Leonard. Dr. Leonard is a personal friend of Al's. He was a member of Al's personal party when the

Governor made a trip through Northern New York at the time he called on President Coolidge just a short time before this investigation. The evidence in the investigation was as damaging to Leonard as to the District Attorney and Sheriff, but executive action was withheld until Leonard had time to resign, which he did. The District Attorney and Sheriff were then removed by the Governor. About six weeks later, after election, when Governor Smith took a trip to Absecon, N. J., with a small party of his closest friends, one of the party was Dr. Leonard, the discredited Saratoga Police Commissioner. Even today, April 29, 1927, as this record is being written, the following appears on the front page of the New York Times: " . . . He made this clear through his friend, Dr. A. J. Leonard, when an effort was made to interview him at the Seaview Golf Club, Absecon, N. J., where he is on a vacation. The Governor declined to be interviewed by newspaper men. He did, however, authorize Dr. Leonard to say . . . ." Incidentally, counsel in the Saratoga investigation offered to show that the Governor had been personally present in some of the most notorious gambling institutions in Saratoga.

Smith's philosophy of prohibition probably is as well summed up in an unguarded statement as in his record, although it would seem that his record spoke for itself.

On March 9, 1923, the New York Times quoted Governor Smith, who had been talking to a reporter about a beer bill introduced in Congress by a New Jersey Senator. The Governor said, according to the New York Times, "I would be glad to go down and help put over his bill if that will get us somewhere where we can put a foot on the rail again and blow off the froth." It is said that he berated and reviled the thoughtless reporter who so quoted him, but the record stood. He had said it, and for once he had not been protected by the press against his own ineptitude.

If "putting a foot on the rail and blowing off the froth" does not mean the saloon, what does it mean? If Smith is not only against prohibition, but in favor of the saloon, how else can his statement be interpreted?

Well, that's Al's record.

CHAPTER III.

RELIGIOUS TOLERANCE.

The opposers of Governor Smith for the Presidency of the United States have thought it wise, he being a Roman Catholic, not to introduce the religious question into the campaign. This is a country of religious liberty, and it is the boast of Protestantism that she always, and everywhere cultivates the spirit of religious tolerance.

But it seems that Mr. Smith's friends are determined to introduce the religious question and try to capitalize a hew and cry against intolerance; for instance, this man Raskob charges Bishop Cannon with opposition to Al Smith because of his being a Roman Catholic, rather than his position with reference to the liquor traffic. Raskob's charge is utterly false. Bishop Cannon has always been a strong advocate of prohibition, has given time and energy to the suppression of the liquor traffic in all of its forms, for many years. He was the most powerful champion and leader of prohibition when Virginia was voted dry. Always and everywhere, with a zeal worthy of the noble, fearless, humanitarian Christian which he is, Bishop Cannon has fought with unflinching courage the brutal, merciless, liquor traffic. He will be remembered long after he has passed away, as the unafraid champion and tireless worker against all of those evils that hinder the uplift and progress of the human race. Of course Raskob is entirely unable to understand or appreciate the sentiments and motives which move a man like Bishop Cannon to the consecration of himself to the welfare of humankind.

Senator Pat Harrison has gone into Mississippi taking up the cudgel for the Roman Catholic Church and in so doing, has brought on an issue that might have, with wisdom, been left out of the campaign, but the Senator having spoken in defense of, and praise for, the Catholic Church, has opened up discussion on a question that has two sides. People having heard one side should by all means hear something of the other side.

It is well known that the Catholic Church is not only a great religious organization, but also a most compact and powerful political body that always has undertaken to control the political life of the nation, where she has had sufficient power to make herself felt in the civic administration of the people.

A distinguished Protestant Bishop sometime ago, stated the fact with reference to this church, very concisely and with great clearness, when he said: "The trouble with the Roman Catholic Church is that it seeks to be both a church and a political party. Its arrogant claims of being the only true Christian church, intolerant as they are, might be treated with indifference; but when for its head it asserts temporal power and civil authority, intruding itself by logical consequence into the political affairs of every country which it enters, a position is assumed which cannot be allowed any church whatsoever. If it must assume such a position, its members must not complain if it is met with political opposition not offered to any other church. This is why such men as Gladstone, Bismarck, Juarez, Diaz, Garibaldi, and the ruling statesmen in France have resisted its pretentions.

"Since the Spanish-American War and the acquisition by the United States of colonies where Romanism has been the established religion, it has been more aggressive than ever in our political affairs. The perils of Romanism to our institutions is not an imaginary danger, conceived by the heated brain of fanatics; it is a real and constant menace. It must be resisted in our country, as it has been resisted in England, Germany, France, Italy, Mexico, Portugal, as it has been resisted in every country where it has secured any considerable following. If it were willing to take its place as a church along with all other churches, it would be improper to meet it with any other attitude than that in which we meet all other churches; but it is not willing to be only a church. Putting itself in a class to itself, by its political animus, it must take all that such an improper position makes inevitable. It cannot claim the political exemption of a church while it asserts such political claims as well as churchly prerogatives."

Lust for temporal power has always characterized the Catholic Church. In her eagerness to control the civil affairs of the people she has sadly neglected their moral, educational, and spiritual welfare. This is plainly manifested in the low moral condition and spiritual dearth in the countries which have been dominated by Romanists for centuries. One of the worst features of the entrance of the Roman Catholic Church into the politics of the United States is the fact that her action makes it absolutely necessary for the Protestant churches of this country to participate in politics as they otherwise would not think of doing, and ought not to be forced to do; but now of necessity should combine all the influences of the various churches who would save this nation from the blight of

Romanism to stand up and stand together in opposition to a wet Roman Catholic who is the advocate and friend of the liquor traffic from his earliest public action to the present moment.

CHAPTER IV.

PROTESTANTISM FORCED INTO POLITICS.

Our Pilgrim Fathers came to this country seeking deliverance from the domination of tyrant kings and persecuting popes. They laid the foundations of a Protestant church, broad and deep, an intellectual and spiritual protest against an infallible pope, robed and mitered priests, a dictatorial and oppressive ecclesiasticism which enslaved the people in ignorance, a religion which largely partook of a pagan idolatry, praying to and worshipping the Virgin Mary, dead saints and their bones; all of this with a fearful state of ignorance and moral depravity which it produced led to a protest, a heart-sick and soul-hunger rebellion against Romanism, with all of its delusions, false views and teachings, with reference to the Bible, the atonement of Christ, and the welfare of human beings in this life and the life to come. Protestant people, then and now, believed that receiving money to pray tortured souls out of purgatory, is the most deceptive and abominable graft that could possibly be perpetrated upon an ignorant and deluded people.

Wherever Romanism has had the power she has always dictated the civic affairs of the nation, and has not hesitated to mass her forces in the political arena against any one who opposed her encroachments and her constant claim to temporal power, which has always made her and, until entirely renounced, must continue to make her a tormenting thorn in the body politic. Wherever she has dominated the political and spiritual forces of the people she has turned the wheels of human progress backward, thought has been stifled, manhood has been dwarfed, pomp and formalism have taken the place of simple humility and spirituality and, in the end, ignorance, superstition and vice have flourished.

Conditions among the masses in Spain, Italy, Mexico, Cuba, the Philippine Islands and South America witness to the full truth of the above statement. As to tolerance, this country had a fine illustration of the utter lack of tolerance, so clearly illustrated in an incident which took place in Rome a few years ago, when Mr. Roosevelt visited that city, and the pope faithfully practiced what he preaches in refusing to receive a call from Mr. Roosevelt, or grant an audience to the ex-president of the United States, because he dared to visit a Protestant Church in Rome, recognize and fellowship with honorable and beloved ministers of the gospel of the Prot-

estant Church, who were not under the domination of the Catholic hierarchy.

Of course, Rome does not undertake force
where force would mean her own destruc-
tion, but she has never failed to use force and
proscription where she has felt it safe to do
so, and her aims and ends could be secured.
Note, for instance, the fact that in the Philippine Islands a Protestant school-teacher is
not permitted to conduct any sort of religious
services in the isolated and spiritual desola-
tion where they teach school or to use any
influence whatsoever that would awaken the
conscience, or win to Christ and his truth,
the souls of their people.

Let it be understood, from first to last, that
we make war on no man, that we do and
must cherish the most kindly and neighborly
feelings toward individual Catholics. We do
warn, however, our people against those
principles, teachings and practices that
would destroy the factors and forces that
have built this great republic and made the
American people the most religious, liberty-
loving, prosperous, and progressive people
in all human history.

It will be remembered that some years
ago, during the life of Cardinal Gibbons, of
Baltimore, he established the practice of go-
ing to St. Patrick's church in Washington

City, on Thanksgiving Day, and holding a Pan-American mass on that day, to which the President of the United States and a large number of other representative politicians of other churches were invited, and they were careful not to refuse to attend said Thanksgiving mass. For them to have done so, would have meant the augmenting of the Catholic vote against them in the various states and districts from which they came.

This yearly Thanksgiving service attended by a large number of Protestant politicians, was kept up until the Protestant ministers of Washington united in the following protest:

"Whereas, For the last three or four years there has been celebrated in St. Patrick's Church in this city on Thanksgiving day, a solemn high mass at which the President of the United States, and some members of his Cabinet, the Chief Justice and several other justices of the Supreme Court, with a number of Senators and members of Congress have attended as the guests of honor; and,—

"Whereas, This service is now called in the public press 'the official celebration of Thanksgiving day,' and is described in the *Bulletin of the Pan-American Republics* as an 'official character,' and every effort is made by the Roman hierarchy to give this

Roman mass the color of an official function,
—as if it were generally recognized as a national service—and as if the President and his Cabinet by their presence wished it to be recognized (which we are sure is not the case) : and,—

"Whereas, One of the papers of the Roman Catholic press (the *Catholic Citizen*, of Milwaukee) states that 'the Pan-American Thanksgiving day high mass is now a permanent institution at the national capital'; and says further, 'One day in the year in which the bountiful Giver of all good things is acknowledged by the nation, as a nation, —this expression of gratitude is made in a Catholic church, around a Catholic altar, by means of the one Catholic worship that is worthy of God, the sacrifice of the mass;' and,—

"Whereas, The attendance of our chief magistrate and members of his Cabinet, not once, but year after year, for four or five years, has been made use of to give color to the Roman claim that this service is now the official celebration of Thanksgiving day in our national capitol; and,—

"Whereas, This fact has been understood, both in the United States and in foreign countries, to give the Roman Catholic Church a prestige and a pre-eminence over all other churches, and has even been believed by people in Brazil and Italy to show that America is not a Protestant but a Roman Catholic country; therefore, be it—

"Resolved, That we protest against the Roman Catholic Church press in putting forward the claims that the Roman mass is 'the official celebration of Thanksgiving day in the capitol of the republic.

"Resolved, That we protest against the attempt to convert our national Thanksgiving day into a Roman Catholic festival, in a service entirely out of harmony with the history and the genius of our country, and the spirit and purpose of the day.

"Resolved, That we desire to give voice to the widespread feeling of indignation among the millions of Protestants of America, against the efforts of the Roman press and the Roman hierarchy to exploit the attendance of our chief magistrate and some of his Cabinet (which we are convinced has not been intended only as an act of courtesy and good will) for the purpose of glorifying the Roman Catholic Church and giving this service an official character, which it does not and cannot possess."

I cannot express the facts with reference

to the Roman Catholic situation in language so clear, correct, and forceful, as it has been done by Rev. Charles E. Jefferson, D.D., one of the most prominent and beloved ministers of New York City. This is taken from "Broadway Tabernacle Tidings."

QUESTION.

"Why are Protestants so prejudiced and so bitter against Roman Catholics?

ANSWER.

"The question is not a fair one because it smuggles into the mind a false assumption. It assumes that all Protestants are prejudiced and bitter. This is not the case. The question should be put in this form: 'Why are so many Protestants prejudiced against Roman Catholics, and why are some of them so bitter?' The answer is that there are various reasons, five of the most important of which are here given:

"I. The Roman Catholic hierarchy maintains an insolent attitude toward the Protestant Church. The Roman Church officially turns her back on us. She gives us the cold shoulder. She refuses to recognize us. She will have nothing to do with us. She denies that we are a true Church at all. We have no place whatever in the real Church of Christ. Our ministers are not successors of

the Apostles. They have no right to officiate
at the Lord's Supper. Our sacraments are
not valid.

"There is only one true Church of Christ in
the world, and the Roman Catholic Church is
it. Many Popes have said this. The present Pope said it again only the other day.
Such conduct awakens resentment. In some
it stirs up bitterness. To Protestants it
seems an odious form of bigotry. So long
as the Roman Catholic Church maintains
this attitude, she is debarred from saying
anything against the bigotry of Protestants.

"II. The Roman Catholic Church officially
refuses to fellowship with Protestants in any
religious council or conference. She will not
allow her bishops and priests to sit down
with Protestant bishops and pastors to talk
over the urgent problems with which the
Church of Christ in our day has to deal. Only
the other day she declined to send even one
delegate to meet in Lausanne with the representatives of the other branches of the Christian Church throughout the world. It was
the greatest Christian conference held in the
last four hundred years, but the Roman
Catholic Church alone refused to have anything to do with it. Such intolerance awakens resentment. It renders some hearts bitter.

"III. The Roman Catholic Church refuses in every community throughout the United States to join with the Protestants in any form of distinctly religious work or worship. All union prayer meetings are ruled out, and so are all union evangelistic campaigns, and so are all union Thanksgiving services, and so are all union Lenten observances. No priest dares to permit his people to unite with Protestants in public prayer. Such snobbishness awakens resentment. It does not work toward good feeling. The surprising thing is not that there is so much anti-Catholic feeling among Protestants, but that there is so little.

"IV. The Roman Catholic hierarchy is the persistent and malignant enemy of the public school system. Roman Catholic bishops and priests and editors and theologians have, during the last fifty years, poured out on our public schools a flood of slander and abuse. Now the public school system is dear to the native American heart. It is counted one of the corner stones of our greatness. We are proud of it. We prize it.

"When Roman Catholic priests year after year use disparaging and insulting language concerning one of our most revered institutions, it is not to be wondered at that the Protestant American heart protests. To read a volume filled with the utterances of prominent Roman Catholics on our public schools is sufficient to set the coldest Protestant heart ablaze.

"This attitude of the priesthood is all the more galling because of the persistent policy of the Roman Catholic Church to shove into our public schools the largest number of Roman Catholic teachers possible. This is one of the sickening inconsistencies of Rome. She calls our schools godless and damnable and vile, and yet assiduously trains thousands of Roman Catholic girls to become teachers in these same ungodly schools.

"There could be no better way to reduce Protestant prejudice against Romanism than for the Pope to call a halt in this everlasting denunciation of our public schools. Catholics obey when orders come from the top, and the fact that this attack on our schools goes steadily on is conclusive proof that the Vatican is willing to have the public schools in the United States incessantly traduced.

"There are few things more wonderful in the American people than their inexhaustible patience in the presence of this pitiless storm of Catholic vituperation against our public schools.

"V. Multitudes of Protestants are afraid of the Roman Catholic Church, because of

what the Popes have said in rgard to the re-
lations of Church and State. The Pope is
called the "Vicar of Christ."   He alone is
supposed to speak for Christ. What he says
is binding on all the faithful. We know
what the Popes have said. Their encyclicals
are public property. These have been re-
printed again and again. Their contents are
well known to all Protestant scholars. They
make serious reading for everyone who be-
lieves in the fundamental principles on which
our Republic is founded.

"A recent volume by Charles C. Marshall,
entitled The Roman Catholic Church in the
Modern State, published by Dodd, Mead &
Company, has brought the most important
of the Papal utterances within the reach of
the ordinary reader. This book is not likely
to reduce the Protestant prejudice against
the Roman Catholic Church.

"When we listen to the Pope we listen to
the Roman Catholic Church. He speaks for
the entire Church. He speaks with authority. He is supreme. The opinions of a Roman Catholic layman in regard to the doc-
trine or government of his Church count for
nothing. He has absolutely nothing to do
with shaping the policy of his Church. The
policy is determined entirely by clergymen.

"The programs are made in Rome. All the

Roman Catholic laymen of the United States are a mere cipher when it comes to deciding what shall be believed and what shall be done. It is because all these highest matters are held tight in the fist of a coterie of Spanish and Italian ecclesiastics that many American Protestants are not at all quiet in their mind in regard to the future."

CHAPTER V.

RUM AND ROMANISM.

With these facts before us can the intelligent, patriotic, citizens of these United States, regardless of party affiliations, take the risk of electing Gov. Al Smith President of the nation? Remember his limitations. His utter unfitness. His advocacy of the liquor traffic. The fact that against the advice of his friends he chose a wet Republican, Roman Catholic, president of his campaign committee. He has been a bold, defiant, sort of man. Elect him President and his conceit and impudence would be tremendously increased. Think of his appointing power. Of the Tammanyites and Wet Catholics he would place in positions of influence and power. Can we, dare we, take such tremendous risk with a man so unfitted and so closely connected with Rum and Romanism?

We regret to be driven to say that the Protestant Church of these United States ought to be aroused and bestir itself, from the greatest Bishop to the humblest and most obscure layman. With no spirit of hatred against any of our fellowbeing, but a genuine love for all the people of the nation. With a courageous advocacy for an open Bible in

every American home, for a free public
school for every American child, and for the
effectual prohibition of the liquor traffic, until it will be as impossible to make, sell, buy,
and use intoxicants illegally, and escape pun-
ishment, as it is to commit murder. Or become an incendiary, and escape the strong
arm of justice.

If there was no disposition to commit
crime there would be no need of laws prohibiting crime. But the depravity of men,
and the inclination to commit crime is such
that laws prohibiting crime must be legisla-
ted. Not only so, but it is understood that
there is always a class of people who will
violate laws. Hence the necessity of penalty
attached to laws. And officials appointed to
inflict these penalties upon the lawless.

Let us stand faithfully by the Eighteenth
Amendment, and strengthen the Volstead
Act. Let Congress pass a law to send out of
this nation all foreigners who for the second
time violate our prohibition law. And con-
fiscation of property, and long periods of im-
prisonment for all home born people who for
the third time violate our prohibition laws.

Elect Al Smith President of these United
States for four years and we will have such
a triumph of the evil forces, and a debauch-
ery of lawlessness as now eixsts in New

York City. Elect him for a second term as President and the Eighteenth Amendment will be eliminated from our Constitution.

If Al Smith should be elected in the coming battle of ballots, the 6th day of next November, I shall be forced to believe that the curse of God has come upon us, because of our spiritual apostasy and reckless lust for wealth and pleasure that has come to characterize such a large per cent of our American people. May the Holy Spirit arouse our womanhood, awaken and stir the manhood of the nation, and may God in mercy save us from a reign of Rum and Romanism.